THE EPISTLE OF JAMES

The Believer and His God: Navigating the Christian Life

BY TAMIA JILL

DORRANCE PUBLISHING CO
EST. 1920
PITTSBURGH, PENNSYLVANIA 15238

Dorrance Publishing Co
585 Alpha Drive
Pittsburgh, PA 15238
Visit our website at *www.dorrancebookstore.com*

ISBN: 979-8-8868-3522-9
eISBN: 979-8-8868- 3610-3

THE EPISTLE OF JAMES

The Believer and His God: Navigating the Christian Life

Introduction

James is an English translation for Jacob—commonly used in the New Testament. While there were various persons with the name—James—this epistle of James was particularly written by James, the brother of Jesus.

James humbly addresses himself in James 1:1 (NKJV) as, "a bond-servant of God and of the Lord Jesus Christ". It was discovered that this James was one of those present with the disciples that waited for the coming of the Holy Spirit—in the upper room. He must have been a deeply spiritual man although there's a record that suggests his previous unbelief in Jesus Christ according to John 7:2-5. Nonetheless, he became a key leader of the Jerusalem Council in Jerusalem—see Acts 15. Besides, the way he heard the argument—listening to various factions and rightly dividing the word of truth—suggests the personality of a responsible man.

James can be rightly considered a man of prayer; hence, you'd notice his much emphasis on prayers in his letter. Paul once referred to him as a pillar in Galatians 2:9. What a great inspiration his life is to present-day Christians, especially when you consider his antecedent—that he failed to believe during Christ's lifetime! James' life inspires and reassures Christ's words to Thomas—blessed are they who don't see but yet believe!

This epistle is said to be written before most of the books in the New Testament. Also, many Bible scholars submit that the epistle of James is symbolic of Jacob's address to his twelve sons—the twelve tribes of Israel. This is because similar to Genesis 49, he wrote: to the twelve tribes which are scattered abroad. Although Israel is often referred to as God's children; likewise, all Christians are spiritual Israelites. So, he wasn't only writing to Jews by birth but to God's chosen people too—all Christians across the world.

The theme of the epistle is undefined, but 'faith' makes a good case. This isn't the saving or justifying faith, but the practical faith manifested in the lifestyles of those yielded to Christ. Touching on a variety of subjects in true Christianity, James emphasizes the need for believers to learn to live for the Lord in every way.

James wrote to the earliest church—people who might have grown accustomed to the religious life of the Old Testament but have now decided to accept Christ. This epistle may equally serve as a guide for those who'd love to be familiar with the person of Jesus. Hence, James describes how the Christian life is an active one—where no one should hide under the subjective reality of faith. He tells how believers must fulfill God's ultimate plan for their lives.

The study of the Bible has always been a journey of discovery—the pursuit of knowledge and many other things for believers. According to 2 Timothy 3:16-17 (NKJV), "All Scripture is given by inspiration of God, and is profitable for doctrine, for reproof, for correction, for instruction in righteousness, that the man of God may be complete, thoroughly equipped for every good work."

It's necessary to always remember that 'the man of God' described in the above verse must be a genuine child of God. James describes who such a genuine child is. Besides, the Lord desires to build the believer—unto maturity and perfect resemblance to Christ. The Epistle of James perfectly describes how true maturity manifests in such a believer too.

James wrote this epistle to the Christian Jews because they were confronted with problems in their personal lives and church fellowship. They experienced stiff trials and temptations, oppression from the rich, and also poverty. It was noted also that their communications weren't gracious—how their tongues set the stage for wars and divisions within the church.

James also aimed to tackle other problems among them like worldliness, willful disobedience to God's word, and double standards of all sorts. Indeed, he described how these problems stemmed from lustful desires and spiritual immaturity.

Unfortunately, among Christians today, spiritual maturity appears to be a far cry. Hence, I've decided to write a breakdown on the teachings of James—to revive believers, remind them about the true Christian life, and sound the clarion call for spiritual maturity!

So, to get the most out of this content, ascertain your spiritual heritage; what's your true state or identity? Are you a Christian or not? Because without a spiritual birth, there can't be spiritual growth: talk less about maturity!

Chapter One
The Christian and His Everyday Life

Our Christian lives may seem complicated to the outside world. Nonetheless, Christianity isn't a mere religion—where you faithlessly follow some rituals and regulations. More than that, it's a religion characterized by a divinely influenced way of life. However, since you don't need to blindly follow rules before you become a Christian, what role must you play?

Well, there are roles to play before and after you're a Christian. The first role is to believe the gospel: to admit and repent that you're a fundamental sinner and Christ paid the debt for your sin, procuring salvation for you. The second role is facilitated by the Holy Spirit given to you when you became a Christian. He teaches you to say 'no' to what God abhors and 'yes' to God's desires. Your role is to be a good student to the Holy Spirit—who does all He prescribes!

If you live in obedience, your life will reveal the nature of Christ, your Savior. The disciples were first called Christians in Antioch—why? People saw their lives. They lived for and like Christ, bearing His identity, daily subjecting the flesh to the spirit, and allowing Christ to rule our lives.

See 2 Corinthians 4:11 (KJV), "For we which live are always delivered unto death for Jesus' sake, that the life also of Jesus might be made manifest in our mortal flesh." So, you'd realize that the disciples had a daily consciousness about living a life that pleased God; in essence, living a life of Jesus.

ENDURING TRIALS AND TEMPTATIONS (2-18)

Many are bewildered that they must be tempted. But temptations are God's way of saying, "I trust you to scale through." Although He doesn't orchestrate temptations, He vests you with grace and stamina to withstand whatever temptations confront you. But not only to withstand them but also to prevail over them.

Remember the book of John, when Jesus had to deal with temptations? God wants us to emulate His demeanor in the face of our trials too. Christ displayed total reliance on the word of God. Like Jesus, temptation and trials are bound to occur. Except we employ reliance on God—as Christ did—could we possibly wriggle our way out? No, only God's power dispels such counter forces.

So, James gives quick advice on what to do when faced with trials. Let's examine them.

JOY

When faced with trials and temptations, don't be crestfallen, giving in to pressure—that's just what the devil would like to see. Instead, be joyful always. Don't just keep the smile on, be truly joyful within. Besides, Christ once said: the student isn't greater than the teacher; if I—the teacher—was treated cruelly and had my fair share of troubles, you will too.

As earlier said, no human can avoid being tempted. But James admonishes that you must see every attempt to be tempted as an opportunity to rejoice. Can the blind tell if there's a ditch ahead? No; so, unbelievers can't be threatened or feel the pressure of temptation; only Christians can sense it. So, rejoice that you can spot the troubles and trials and subsequently avoid or prevail over them.

Also, consider Nehemiah 8:10 (NLT), "And Nehemiah continued, 'Go and celebrate with a feast of choice foods and sweet drinks, and share gifts of food with people who have nothing prepared. This is a sacred day before our Lord. Don't be dejected and sad, for the joy of the LORD is your strength!'" Indeed, don't let anything put out your fire as you rejoice in the Lord daily. Be rather conscious that God's joy is your strength in trying times. He'd not allow temptations you can't withstand to cross your path!

PATIENCE

In the face of trials, you need tons of patience. You must be resilient and ready to endure whatever situation you find yourself in. When you're attuned to God's Spirit, relying on His faithfulness and sure deliverance from every circumstance, you can exercise true patience. Besides, since you're exercising patience because you must endure persecution in your Christian life, a reward is sure. See Hebrews 10:35 (NLT), "Do not throw away this confident trust in the Lord, no matter what happens. Remember the great reward it brings you!"

Besides, as your reliance based on God's integrity—faith—is tested, patience will grow. If only you endure until help arrives, your next interaction with such situations will be less turbulent. That's why it's written in James 1:3-4 (NLT), "For when your faith is tested, your endurance has a chance to grow. So let it grow, for when your endurance is fully developed, you will be strong in character and ready for anything."

GOD'S WISDOM

Wisdom is a topic you can't afford to take at face value. It's similar to Christ's record about peace. He said, "Peace I leave with you, my peace I give to you: not as the world gives, give I to you. Let not your heart be troubled, neither let it be afraid." If Christ's kind of peace isn't the world's kind, you should know that God's wisdom isn't human wisdom—they're different!

The Bible often remarks that awe and reverence for God are the best basis for wisdom. This implies that you must be undergirded by a divine consciousness as you decide on all matters. Likewise, James describes how to obtain such wisdom. However, he starts by clearing your doubts about God's disposition to those who seek divine wisdom. He reassures his readers that God wouldn't chastise them for seeking wisdom. Instead, He's on hand to give it to you in abundance. See James 1:5 (KJV), "if any of you lacks wisdom, let him ask of God, who giveth liberally and without reproach."

However, since the need for wisdom highlights your admittance to be insufficient—one way or another—James explains that you must approach God as the only choice you have. Until you come to the point where you're not wavering, expect no help or slice of wisdom from God! The Bible describes this same reality in Hebrews 11:6 (NLT), "So, you see, it is impossible to please God without faith. Anyone who wants to come to him must believe that there is a God and that he rewards those who sincerely seek him."

Although James later shed more light on the nature of God's wisdom—how it manifests and is outrightly different from human wisdom—he reproves and encourages the faint-hearted. So, if you must know what God would have you do, your mind must be set like flint as described in Isaiah 50:7 (NLT), "Because the Sovereign LORD helps me, I will not be dismayed. Therefore, I have set my face like a stone, determined to do his will. And I know that I will triumph."

RIGHT PERSPECTIVE

Consider the bolts of lightning that appear in the sky—how electric and flashy they can be. Do you realize how starkly bright they appear in the night too? Yes, they may be bright and electric, but can they be relied on as a credible source of electricity and light; can the world consider them? No. Why not? Because they're unstable and unpredictable and that makes them very unpleasant and scary to many.

Similarly, some are as unstable as the lightning and can't be relied upon. How can this set of people expect anything from God? Besides, how can they form a standard perspective if they're always wavering and changing sides at every turn of events? Indeed, they can be more treacherous than the wind and may even hide under the shadow of 'being liberal'. But the truth remains: they're disturbed, lack inner peace, and have a skewed outlook on life at large.

What's more, their worldview is outrageously amenable because they tend to be 'laissez-faire' with an undertone of nonchalance. This is what their wavering mind as made of them—they're incapable of having a perspective, talk less about the right perspective. James mentioned this and I decided to give an insightful detail into it. However, you should know that an unwavering mind has more chances of subscribing to the 'right divine perspective'.

SOURCES OF TEMPTATION

The desires of the flesh.
Some can't help but satisfy their craving for a bar of chocolate even if it threatens their health. They may begin with some negotiation to only have one bar but eventually they get two, three, and even become insatiable. Human nature is modeled to crave things, especially when they give us pleasure. James describes how your temptation is only a product of your lustful desires.

Many hold the belief that temptations are God's way of testing them—that God initiates temptation. They make others feel spiritually inferior because they battle some temptations, and even boast about their superior intimacy with God because they conquered temptations of some sort. Not only don't we find in the Bible—where God's love and intimacy are based on what we do or don't do—but James sets the record straight.

The doctrine above isn't only misleading but reveals the deep-seated vanity in the hearts of many—their lust for superiority. Notwithstanding, see James 1:13-16 (NLT), "And remember, no one who wants to do wrong should ever say, 'God is tempting me.' God is never tempted to do wrong, and he never tempts anyone else either. Temptation comes from the lure of our own evil desires. These evil desires lead to evil actions, and evil actions lead to death. So don't be misled, my dear brothers and sisters."

James procures a solution for those battling temptations. He illuminates them and weaponized them with the knowledge that can help them in their battles. And what's this knowledge? That you need help; that you're the weak link for the invasion of temptations. And to those who lust for superiority, James delivers a humbling blow—that they're wrong and if anything, self-righteousness will keep them farther from God. Indeed, God hates the proud but gives grace to the humble!

So, how do you tame the flesh and its desires? First, remember Christ's words in Mark 8:34 (NLT), "Then he called his disciples and the crowds to come over and listen. 'If any of you wants to be my follower,' he told them, 'You must put aside your selfish ambition, shoulder your cross, and follow me.'"

Your mind is renewed when you give ears to the Holy Spirit's renewal program. Besides, this program is only carried out by God's rightly interpreted word in the Bible. So, the Bible admonishes you not to be conformed to this world but to be renewed to understand God's desires at all times. Indeed, following the step of God's word is one way to escape the scathing booby trap that the flesh and its lust relentlessly set.

Expressly, see Galatians 5:24-25 (NLT), "Those who belong to Christ Jesus have nailed the passions and desires of their sinful nature to his cross and crucified them there. If we are living now by the Holy Spirit, let us follow the Holy Spirit's leading in every part of our lives." This much information settles it!

Love for the things of the world.
"Watch and pray, that ye enter not into temptation: the spirit indeed is willing, but the flesh is weak." This is one of the most profound calls to today's Christian. Christ yet gives full disclosure on how far your

supposed determination and discipline will go in matters like this if you're not divinely empowered. Christ implies that those who don't have God's Spirit are indeed helpless in the face of these battles. But the same fate awaits the Christian who doesn't acknowledge and yield to God's Spirit. According to Christ, when you don't yield, you may as well rely on the 'already weak flesh'.

I already mentioned that the flesh remains the weak link if it's not subjected to daily crucifixion as you yield to the prevailing power of the Holy Spirit. The flesh can't help itself; it always gives in to temptation! The flesh can't conquer the world. Besides, see how the Bible describes what's in the world in 1 John 2:16 (NLT), "For the world offers only the lust for physical pleasure, the lust for everything we see, and pride in our possessions. These are not from the Father. They are from this evil world."

Again, what's God's solution to this? The Bible indicates those that can defeat the world. See 1 John 5:4-5 (NLT), "For every child of God defeats this evil world by trusting Christ to give the victory. And the ones who win this battle against the world are the ones who believe that Jesus is the Son of God." So, only the child with the love of the Father can prevail over love for the world. Are you God's child; do you believe that Jesus is God's Son; are you saved? It's the only way to record victory over the world and its desires.

GOODNESS FROM THE FATHER OF LIGHT

Have you realized that although mankind continues to make groundbreaking progress in several ways and sectors, they're yet unable to do anything outside some principles in the universe? Instead, mankind so understands the immutability of such principles and rather makes them the bedrock of much breathtaking innovation. These principles are referred to as 'the laws of nature'.

Two of such principles are gravitational and electromagnetic force. But, why do you need to know these as we discuss the goodness of God?

Well, since physical laws like these principles can't be outrightly manipulated or compromised, why do people misconceive the nature of God's goodness? If these principles are immutable, beyond them, God's goodness is too—God doesn't do evil.

The scriptures drove this point home as they discussed how, instead of tempting people or tripping people up with evil lusts, God is impervious to evil in James 1:13, 16-17 (NLT), "And remember, no one who wants to do wrong should ever say, 'God is tempting me.' God is never tempted to do wrong, and he never tempts anyone else either. So don't be misled, my dear brothers and sisters. Whatever is good and perfect comes to us from God above, who created all heaven's lights. Unlike them, he never changes or casts shifting shadows."

If as a matter of divine principle, God never does evil, it's then proper to discuss the nature of God's goodness. I've revealed in the above lines that His goodness is immutable. Since God has no beginning or end and preexists the world, then His nature must have the same features. Hence, His goodness preexists the world too. No one asked for Him to be good or sought after His goodness, especially after the fall when mankind became alienated from Him and His desires.

God's goodness is so immutable that it reveals many of His virtues to both believers and unbelievers. Jesus revealed this in Matthew 5:45 (NLT), "In that way, you will be acting as true children of your Father in heaven. For he gives his sunlight to both the evil and the good, and he sends rain on the just and on the unjust too."

Similarly, just as He ordered the sun and rain to reveal His goodness to everyone, He procured salvation for everyone too. Truth is, Christ is the true sun and rain that shines and falls on every kind of person today. He's the sun of righteousness to as many that believe in His death and resurrection. He's likewise the unceasing showers of rain and water that seeks to quench everyone who thirsts.

There's plenty to describe but do you see how immutable God's goodness is; do you realize how it also conveys the gift of eternal life to those that believe? Indeed, Christ is the goodness of God and He's the preacher of the same; see Luke 4:18 -19 (NLT), "'The Spirit of the Lord is upon me, for he has appointed me to preach Good News to the poor. He has sent me to proclaim that captives will be released, that the blind will see, that the downtrodden will be freed from their oppressors, and that the time of the Lord's favor has come.'"

TRUE RELIGION

There's a present-day complication on the topic of religion, especially among Christians. Some are quick to say, "Christianity isn't a religion; it's a way of life." Although this is because they perceive that religion always has undertones of rituals, are they correct in their submission?

Let's examine what religion means in the pure English language. According to Wikipedia, "Religion is usually defined as a social-cultural system of designated behaviors and practices, morals, beliefs, world-views, texts, sanctified places, prophecies, ethics, or organizations, that generally relates humanity to supernatural, transcendental, and spiritual elements."

Look at the above definition and realize that Christianity possesses every feature above. In Christianity, although influenced by the Holy Spirit and God's rightly interpreted word, we're yet commanded to behave in a way, practice some things, believe and never despise prophecies, worship in order and not confusion, and many more. Besides, since other religions exist and have their practices too, Christianity is a worldview.

But what's a worldview? It's a collection of attitudes, values, stories, and expectations about the world around us. These things inform our every thought and action! Since we've debunked the position held by those who try so hard to not make Christianity a religion, let's now see how James describes true religion.

Hearing the word of God.

The book of James emphasizes 'hearers of the word'. As a growing child, hearing the words of your parents should produce certain reactions. Consider your parents' words—their words when you make them proud, sad, or even their words of encouragement. Don't you think they played a role in who you are today? Similarly, the word of God is impactful to our souls.

Let's consider some impactful statements in James, ones you'd be expected to put into action. How do you compose yourself when you're quizzed on what you might not have done? Do you get overly anxious, defensive, and vindictive against those who bring a matter against you? Well, here's what the scriptures will have you do, according to James 1:19-20 (NLT), "My dear brothers and sisters, be quick to listen, slow to speak, and slow to get angry. Your anger can never make things right in God's sight."

Another statement is: don't just listen to God's word, do it! James called anyone who hears God's word but doesn't do what He says a deceitful person—only that such a person wouldn't only be deceiving others but themselves too. So, how often do you meditate and apply what you've read in the Bible to yourself? Do you even realize that it's hypocritical to hear a thing, say one thing, and do another?

Finally, Paul describes his Christian life, explaining how what he teaches—says—is the same thing he does—acts. See 1 Thessalonians 1:5 (NLT), "For when we brought you the Good News, it was not only with words but also with power, for the Holy Spirit gave you full assurance that what we said was true. And you know that the way we lived among you was further proof of the truth of our message."

A bridled tongue:

We're in a world where the line between 'acceptable and unacceptable' continues to be blurred. People are becoming lovers of self and now try to assert their thoughts and beliefs whether it affects another person or not. The yardstick of 'truth' is faced with fierce conflict and people would rather live by 'personalized truths'. But try as they might, they can't do anything against the truth but for it!

The same is true about the Christian religion. Although false teachers are in their numbers and enjoy more media visibility, the truth of the Christian religion—though not widely accepted— will prevail! One of the truths of Christianity is our speech. It's an aspect that's played down and becoming secularized. However, we forget that the Bible describes that 'out of the abundance of the heart, the mouth speaks'.

Many pay little or no attention to this reality and live unguided, speaking without a guard. But James explains that true religion means that our words should always be seasoned with the salt of grace. Indeed, every word that comes from your mouth should inspire hope and life; they must be words of encouragement and upliftment. Undoubtedly, Christianity loses its value if we can't control our tongue!

How well Christians guard their speech reveals how mature they are. You're not to be a slave to your emotions and circumstances. See James 1:26 (NLT), "If you claim to be religious but don't control your tongue, you are just fooling yourself, and your religion is worthless."

Understanding the power of the tongue and its right usage is important. Do you know that Jesus rebuked the 'sons of thunder' because they didn't understand the kind of power a true Christian possesses? See Luke 9:54-56 (NKJV), "And when His disciples James and John saw this, they said, 'Lord, do You want us to command fire to come down from heaven and consume them, just as Elijah did?' But He turned and rebuked them, and said, 'You do not know what manner of spirit you are of. For the Son of Man did not come to destroy men's lives but to save them.' And they went to another village."

Helping the helpless.
The book of James emphasizes care. Caring for others in their distress. You must have a heart of compassion; a heart that feels pity and helps

others. Besides, Mathew 5:7 says, "Blessed are the merciful, for they shall obtain mercy." Hence, true religion sympathizes with others. It also sees the need to offer prayers, financial help, and word of encouragement. Indeed, true Christianity reflects God's unconditional love.

Finally, true religion implies that you love what God loves and hate what He hates. It means you don't call 'evil' good, or 'good' evil! Besides, love for the Father and love for the world can't dwell in the same heart. So, true religion is to love the Father because He first loved you! Consequently, the last verse in the first chapter of James says: pure and undefiled religion before God and the Father is this—to visit orphans and widows in their trouble, and to keep oneself unspotted from the world.

Chapter Two
The True Christian Faith

"But without faith, it is impossible to please Him: for he that cometh to God must believe that he is and that he is a rewarder of them that diligently seek him".

- Hebrews 11:6

When I consider creation, I burst out in praise for God who put everything in place and holds them with His power. The sun, moon, land, water bodies, mountains, valleys, plants, animals, and many more are a work of art and I'm amazed when I see them in action. However, these are just a portion of what God has created. I dare to say that God has created things that haven't crossed the mind of any human being, especially because these things are outside the planet earth.

What does this mean? I'm driving at the point where you'd realize that every created thing in existence was done by Him. These include the cosmos, galaxies, milky-way, atoms, satellites, and even planets. Yes, planets! You might not realize it before now, but I ask, "Who do you think created the planets?" Indeed, God did. And it's not improper or illogical to understand that while Scientists have confirmed that the earth appears to be tailor-made for human beings, they're not that informed about the peculiarity of other planets.

While they may only evaluate the viability of other planets based on their ability to be mankind's second or third planet of habitation, God who created all planets must have more reasons for creating them. Besides, He's the only one who knows why they exist, Scientists can only remain inquisitive. But since they've been able to gather some information about them, how do these Scientists reach other planets? Do they go by water, road, or merely by air?

Have you heard about Elon musk? He owns a company that seeks to make spaceflight affordable. Space or other planets can't be accessed via road, water, or merely by air. The aircraft that journey around the earth can't make it to space. Yes, the normal jets, choppers, and planes can't do the job and part of the problem is the Earth's gravity. You need to escape it to reach space and it requires a minimum speed of Mach 33—25,000 mph. However, the current world record for the fastest plane is only Mach 6.7—5,140 mph.

Besides, the other problem is the atmosphere. As you fly higher, the atmosphere grows thinner. This creates two serious issues: one, fewer air molecules mean it's harder for the plane to stay airborne. Two: less oxygen means less combustible fuel to power the engine. So, without the spaceflight designed to journey into space and planets, nothing else can do the job. That's where I'm coming to concerning this discussion of faith!

Consider the space and all the creation in it at the moment as 'God'. Take the spaceflight that's designed to enter the space as 'faith'. Indeed, without faith, no one can have access to God! And that's just how God has Sovereignly designed it. God's not partial and He interacts with everyone and anyone that has faith in His Son. However, no natural man is inclined to God or designed to naturally believe Him. So, the gift to believe, to have faith, is from Him!

Isn't it awesome to realize that God gives you and me the vehicle to make it into His space for free? More amazingly, He has ensured that there are no double standards. The truth is there's only one standard and it's His Christ. His Christ distributes faith to as many that give ears to the gospel. Remember that the Bible says: faith comes by hearing the word of God! Now, what did James say about this faith?

FAITH AND IMPARTIALITY

Since Christ's death made faith attainable and consequently salvation, isn't it right to know who Christ's death is effective towards? There was a scuffle on this matter in the earliest Church. The apostles questioned the rationale behind the gospel being preached to the gentiles. But Paul and Peter narrated their experiences about how God baptized the gentiles with the Holy Spirit, in the exact way even they were baptized on the day of Pentecost.

You should remember Peter's religious stance after he saw a vision where God commanded Him to eat unclean animals. Well, God schooled him in the same vision saying, "Nothing is unclean." This vision was to let Peter know that he and other Jewish-Christians were permitted to enter the homes of the Gentiles—whom they considered unclean— to bring them the Good News of Jesus Christ. It reveals that indeed, Christ's faith and salvation is for all, even the worst sinner.

The Christian faith is evidently built on God's impartial nature and James spoke on how Christians fail to act in the same way. James tackled Christians and their propensity to be impartial, giving more advantage to the wealthy over the poor. This was an aberrant behavior, strange to true Christianity and unfortunately, it's still in vogue in present-day churches. Anyone who understands the basis of Christianity and how they became children of God must not behave partially.

What about you; are you impartial? Do you pander to favoritism? See James 2:1-4 (NLT), "My dear brothers and sisters, how can you claim that you have faith in our glorious Lord Jesus Christ if you favor some people more than others? For instance, suppose someone comes into your meeting dressed in fancy clothes and expensive jewelry, and another comes in who is poor and dressed in shabby clothes. If you give special attention and a good seat to the rich person, but you say to the poor one, 'You can stand over there, or else sit on the floor'—well, doesn't this discrimination show that you are guided by wrong motives?"

THE BLUEPRINT OF IMPARTIALITY!

Galatians 3: 26, 28 (NLT) says, "So you are all children of God through faith in Christ Jesus. There is no longer Jew or Gentile, slave or free, male or female. For you are all Christians—you are one in Christ Jesus." There's no other blueprint or template any Christian must look up to except Christ! His ministry on earth is replete with fairness and justice.

He even tackled the teachers of the law for not emphasizing the same, according to Matthew 23:23 (NLT), "How terrible it will be for you teachers of religious law and you Pharisees. Hypocrites! For you are careful to tithe even the tiniest part of your income, but you ignore the important things of the law—justice, mercy, and faith. You should tithe, yes, but you should not leave undone the more important things."

Christ frowns at the kind of Christian faith that doesn't reflect fair and honest interactions with others. You'd remember how He humbly and equally washed the feet of His disciples and taught them to do the same? Indeed, He's the perfect example for every Christian who desires godly living.

Throughout His ministry on earth, He was always impartial. Although some people point to how He often chose only three disciples—Peter, James, and John—to accompany Him on important occasions. Indeed, He took them to the mountain of Transfiguration and also to Gethsemane, but this wasn't about partiality. On the Mount of Transfiguration, they were there as witnesses and because He didn't want everyone to know who He was yet, He took only three disciples with Him but warned them about whatever they saw, according to Matthew 17:8 -9 (NLT), "And when they looked, they saw only Jesus with them. As they descended the mountain, Jesus commanded them, 'Don't tell anyone what you have seen until I, the Son of Man, have been raised from the dead.'"

It's only logical to consider that if He took more disciples along to the Mount of Transfiguration, there'd be lesser chances of what they saw remaining a secret until after His death. Then at Gethsemane, the Bible revealed that it was a garden known to all the disciples. However, Jesus revealed to all His disciples that He'd be taken from them that night. So, it's only understandable again that He only took three disciples with Himself because there was no real need to bring them all along. Remember that He said, "Strike the shepherd and the sheep will scatter." So, there's no indication in the entire gospels that He only took three disciples with Himself because He loved them more than others or preferred them to others.

Besides, you might argue that the gospel refers to John as the disciple whom the Master mostly loved. But Jesus' words and perception of the disciples are scattered especially in the sixteenth and seventeenth chapters of the gospel of John. Catch a glimpse here in John 17:12, 21 (NLT), "During my time here, I have kept them safe. I guarded them so that not one was lost, except the one headed for destruction, as the Scriptures foretold. My prayer for all of them is that they will be one, just as you and I are one, Father—that just as you are in me and I am in you, so they will be in us, and the world will believe you sent me."

Beyond any gainsaying, do you see the equal divine pedestal Christ placed all of His disciples? Impartiality is God's way and even when He does things that mere men consider to be impartial, remember that only God judges and evaluates things, you don't have such liberty. Hence, isn't it a step too far, to try to measure God's deeds, especially when you know that you're limited in knowledge and wisdom? Indeed, it's an absolute reality that God's not only just, He's justice, and He's not only always fair but He's fairness personified!

Reasons not to show partiality

God's value system is sovereign. Until you acknowledge this, you might continue to question His actions. While He doesn't want you and me to be partial in our interactions with others, He might do things that you might consider as partiality. But with God, many things—that we might have no idea about—might constitute His unquestionable decisions.

Hence, James focused on your interactions with fellow humans and not about God's interactions with them. James sternly urged that partiality be shunned totally by Christians. He described how the mindset that tends to support one person over the other isn't one influenced by the Holy Spirit.

Since this decision to favor one person over the other is often beclouded by many lustful factors, you'd realize that partiality is an expression of the works of the flesh. It even reveals the immaturity of such a Christian—who lives by sight and would rather dance to the tune of the wealthy at the cost of the poor. Some would rather grant access to Christians who are well-dressed and keep the ones in tatters away from themselves.

This work of the flesh isn't only found in the places of worship but everywhere and you must be on guard to shun it and rather pander to the desire of the Holy Spirit. With the Holy Spirit alone can you be impartial. Without Him, you're vulnerable and will only carry out the desires of the flesh. Consider James 2:9 (NLT), "But if you pay special attention to the rich, you are committing a sin, for you are guilty of breaking that law."

Also, impartiality can quickly mean that you're not merciful to the poor. A partial person is practically merciless; they don't care enough about the consequences that may befall those they've deprived. Many times, what they think about is how to be in the good books of a prominent person. Unfortunately, they incur God's judgment when they do so, according to James 2:13 (NLT), "For there will be no mercy for you if you have not been merciful to others. But if you have been merciful, then God's mercy toward you will win out over his judgment against you."

You must shun this attitude because like every sin, it puts you on the fast lane to becoming a wayward Christian. And soon, your quest to please the people who are better placed will lure you outside God's purview. This isn't a good thing because the Bible says in Hebrews 10:30-31 (NLT), "For we know the one who said, 'I will take vengeance. I will repay those who deserve it.' He also said, 'The Lord will judge his own people.' It is a terrible thing to fall into the hands of the living God."

FAITH AND WORKS

James emphasizes the fact that faith without work is useless. Now, what's the work? Work in this context does not mean occupation or profession. What James means is that faith must be lived out for people to see; not only to be practiced in the heart. You'd remember that Christ urges the same in Matthew 5:14-16 (NLT), "You are the light of the world—like a city on a mountain, glowing in the night for all to see. Don't hide your light under a basket! Instead, put it on a stand and let it shine for all. In the same way, let your good deeds shine out for all to see, so that everyone will praise your heavenly Father."

Besides, a practical example is on display in the book of James. Some Christians aren't aware of the trouble of seemingly living in isolation and leading unproductive lives. James 2:14-17 (NLT) explains, "Dear brothers and sisters, what's the use of saying you have faith if you don't prove it by your actions? That kind of faith can't save anyone. Suppose you see a brother or sister who needs food or clothing, and you say, 'Well, good-bye and God bless you; stay warm and eat well'—but then you don't give that person any food or clothing. What good does that do? So you see, it isn't enough just to have faith. Faith that doesn't show itself by good deeds is no faith at all—it is dead and useless."

The Christian faith leads to action and history proves it. Whether Old Testament or New, believers are known to the outside world by their faith-influenced actions. Even today, people like William Tyndale, George Whitefield, William Wilberforce, Michael Faraday, Frances Willard, Christian Führer, Billy Graham, and many more. Don't hesitate to read about their accomplishments in furthering God's word and reality across the world.

THOSE WHO BACKED FAITH WITH WORKS.

Abraham

God said unto Abraham in Genesis 22:2 "…take now thy son, thine only son Isaac, whom thou lovest, and get thee into the land of Moriah; and offer him there for a burnt offering upon one of the mountains which I will tell thee of." Abraham obediently released his son to God not knowing that it was a test. Although he had faith in God, his works proved it.

Similarly, sometimes, what you're experiencing might only require some ounces of work. Until you've done the work, faith isn't considered to be alive, according to James 2:22-23 (NLT), "You see, he was trusting God so much that he was willing to do whatever God told him to do. His faith was made complete by what he did—by his actions. And so, it happened just as the Scriptures say: 'Abraham believed God, so God declared him to be righteous.' He was even called 'the friend of God.'"

THE LAD

The Bible didn't say anything about this boy except for his single act of kindness to others. He surrendered his fish and bread without thinking he was going to go hungry that day. This is faith in action in the life of this lad. Jesus collected the food and blessed it, and the bread and fish increased. People ate and some leftovers occupied twelve baskets. Indeed, working out your faith fearlessly makes one's life a blessing to others.

The widow at Zarephath

This widow gave up her last meal to Elijah without looking back. At first, she told Elijah, "As the LORD thy God liveth, I have not a cake, but a handful of meal in a barrel, and a little oil in a cruse: and behold, I am gathering two sticks, that I may go in and dress it for me and my son, that we may eat it and die." Eventually, she obeyed Elijah by first preparing his meal. This is the faith at work, she didn't tell Elijah she was going to think about it. In return, she enjoyed the miracle of an overflow—her oil didn't run out, and neither did her bread!

The maid of Naaman's wife

This girl didn't hesitate to offer help to the captain because she was captured by the Syrian host. This teaches us that even in difficult or uncomfortable interactions, especially with our enemies, we should demonstrate faith with works. She encouraged her master, Naaman, to go dip himself in the Jordan River as directed by the prophet Elisha. To a large extent, you can attribute Naaman's cleansing to her persistence.

Rahab the prostitute

Rahab was a prostitute, but she was recognized by God for her kind act towards the spies that came to Jericho. She didn't sell them out in a bid to keep enjoying the city they would soon destroy. Instead, knowing that they were Israelites, she hid them from harm's way. She could have died while doing so if she was caught. So, despite being a prostitute, she risked her life for others; what an act of true faith! This isn't to encourage anyone to express actions in faith while living in sin. No, but acts of faith rather prove that we're righteous and heed to God's desires.

Finally, it's compulsory to have faith that produces good works. Christ wants you and me to do the same and warns about the fate that'd befall those who don't in John 15:2-4 (NLT), "He cuts off every branch that doesn't produce fruit, and he prunes the branches that do bear fruit so they will produce even more. You have already been pruned for greater fruitfulness by the message I have given you. Remain in me, and I will remain in you. For a branch cannot produce fruit if it is severed from the vine, and you cannot be fruitful apart from me." Always remember that you can only bear fruit when you reside in Him; without Him, you can't do a dime!

Chapter Three
Christian Wisdom

"If you would pass for more than your value, say little.
It is easier to look wise than to talk wisely."

- Thomas Fuller

James continues his epistle by dealing largely with two crucial phenomena: wisdom and words. He makes sure to pass the message that uncontrolled words and worldly wisdom could and can account for a man's downfall. This means that the meaning of both words is rather too important to ignore. In case you thought the "most valuable part" of your body was your brain that processes a mindboggling range of thousands of ideas every day; or your heart that just keeps doing the amazing second-by-second job of pumping blood throughout your body, James gives a rude awakening by writing, "For we all stumble in many things. If anyone does not stumble in word, he is a perfect man, able also to bridle the whole body." (vs. 2 NKJV).

The bottom line, according to him, is that the tongue is the most extraordinarily powerful and uncontrollable part of your body! If you could completely control your words, you would have completely gained mastery over your entire body and by extension, your life. Isn't it strange that James compares this little pink muscle to the fire of hell? What more understanding would you then need to know that your tongue is not at the same impact level as any other organ of your body?

In a way, he also revealed that this matter concerned everyone except someone nested safely in the arms of perfection. His point wasn't perfection but that we all carried the burden of taming the tongue. Where does wisdom come in? "...He who restrains his lips is wise." (Proverbs 10:19 NKJV). That's right, wisdom is seen when you tame your tongue.

UNDERESTIMATED DANGER

Let's take a peek at how dangerous the tongue actually is. James writes, "And the tongue is a fire, a world of iniquity. The tongue is so set among our members that it defiles the whole body, and sets on fire the course of nature; and it is set on fire by hell." Isn't it interesting how we pay more attention to dangers such as death, diseases, war, famine, global warming, terrorism, and so on and sideline the most underestimated danger of all: the tongue?

Don't be surprised because, in one of the most known scriptures of the Bible, Solomon said, "Death and life are in the power of the tongue, and those who love it will eat its fruit." Wow! Death, the end of all things, and life, the beginning of all things are both controlled by this tiny pink muscle in the mouth. When Jesus said that His words were spirit and life, it meant for a fact that the tongue was definitely the major instrument He used in shaping this world forever; He is the greatest teacher of all time!

When you see people talk any way they like, it's because they've underestimated the danger the tongue can pose to any cadre of people. Sooner or later, evil words spoken tend to manifest. Don't be like people who aren't aware of who don't care that the tongue is dangerous. The fact that it was compared to small but extremely important things like the bits on a horse's mouth, the rudder that's used to stir a massive ship, and a seemingly tiny spark that can set an entire forest ablaze says it all!

DAMAZO!

"Learn to hold thy tongue; five words cost Zacharias forty weeks of silence."

- Thomas Fuller

'Damazo' is Greek for 'tame', and it means 'to crush'; 'subdue'; 'depress'; 'to make spiritless, gentle or meek'. Do you know you wield a great force of power every time your lips move with words (an average of 700 times per day) being produced? Well, you do! Although James did not clearly state the benefits of using the tongue well, he laid a foundation. Good words have the power to uplift, encourage and inspire people and even you the speaker. Bad words on the other hand can crush a heart, cause division, or cause you or your listeners to despair.

Saying the wrong things cause terrible pains and discomfort, especially when spoken at sensitive atmosphere; imagine someone saying out loud at a funeral about the deceased, "He wasn't really worth anything. Why waste my tears?" No matter how true that may have been in reality, those words aren't something the family and loved ones of the deceased would want to ever hear, right? So how do you tame the tongue to speak the right words? How do you bring it under subjection? Is it easy to do? Is it beneficial? James wrote, "out of the same mouth proceed blessing and cursing. My brethren, these things ought not to be so." (vs. 10 NKJV).

The major ways that are recommended to keep your tongue "damazoed" are protecting the powerhouse, that is the heart (Proverbs 4:23) because like James writes, "Does a spring send forth fresh water and bitter from the same opening?" (vs. 11 NKJV); digging into the Word (2 Corinthians 3:18); partnering with the Holy Spirit (Galatians 5:26); and of course, spending quality time in prayers (Luke 18:1). By doing these consistently, your tongue will conform to the way the very tongue of Christ Himself is: tamed!

Consistency helps because it is a difficult thing to do; imagine keeping quiet as led by the Spirit when you're hurt or saying "thank you" to someone who evidently disrespects you. Taming your tongue is most difficult in environments such as the home when your spouse says or does something annoying like making decisions that would affect the entire household without your input or your children being naughty. What about the workplace where some of your employees or colleagues may have little or no regard for you? As a teacher, have you found it hard to hold your words when students misbehave? As a minister, when people say demeaning things about you, don't you feel like giving them a piece of your mind? Why do you need to restrain yourself? It's because the Holy Spirit is there to help. It's high time you partner with Him to keep your tongue subjected; your slave, not you being its slave!

THE RIGHT APPLICATION OF KNOWLEDGE

> "As we trust God to give us wisdom for today's decisions, He will lead us a step at a time into what He wants us to be doing in the future."
>
> -Theodore Epp

Oxford says of wisdom that it is the "capacity of judging rightly in matter relating to life and conduct; soundness of judgment in the choice of means and ends; sometimes, less strictly, sound sense, especially in practical affairs; it is the opposite of folly". What all these words point at is the fact that wisdom is the word used to describe an act done in accordance with the right information and knowledge.

Interesting, there are different kinds of wisdom that exist. James proves it by writing, "This wisdom does not descend from above, but is earthly, sensual, demonic." (vs. 15 NKJV). You're definitely well acquainted with human wisdom even if it's not the best. Why? Human wisdom always clashes with God's wisdom. It's a reason why there's so many heartaches in the world right now. When you take actions solely based on your knowledge and not God's foresight, you're most likely to fall into traps and hurtful situations. But when you give God space to lead you in His wisdom that may not make sense to you, you'll always be victorious. But what exactly are these types of wisdom and how do they affect your life and the lives of others around you?

HUMAN OR EARTHLY WISDOM

The wisdom of this era is based on knowledge gotten from books, experiences and observations. Anyone, whether or not they have the Holy Spirit, can gain this wisdom. You don't need the Holy Spirit to attend a prestigious medical school or law school to become a doctor or lawyer. This kind of wisdom is dependent largely on tradition, education and reasoning.

It is this type of wisdom that makes people think they're successful solely because of their intelligence or wittiness in business or some other sphere of influence. Human wisdom doesn't give God glory nor acknowledge the influence of God. Although human wisdom is good and all, it fades at the sight of both Godly wisdom and demonic wisdom.

DEMONIC WISDOM

If you weren't told, you may never have agreed that demons too are wise. What is a demonic wisdom? It is any wisdom that opposes or suspends the wisdom of God. It is inspired and sponsored by the devil himself. For example, it is demonic to think that same-sex marriage is okay; it is demonic to think that anything God says can be tweaked to suit you even if that was not the aim of God's Word. It is demonic wisdom that begins the steps towards such evils as thefts, prostitutions, murders, terrorisms, etc.

GODLY WISDOM

To round off this chapter, James writes, "but the wisdom that is from above is first pure, then peaceable, gentle, willing to yield, full of mercy and good fruits, without partiality and hypocrisy." (vs. 17). As opposed to human wisdom, Godly wisdom does not originate from books or by observations or experiences; Godly wisdom comes from spiritual discernment sponsored by the Spirit of God.

GODLY WISDOM VS HUMAN WISDOM

When God speaks a word of healing to you or a loved one for example, what first counters the word of wisdom isn't demonic but human. Why? Medical materials, experiences, observations and even people will influence you to think it's farfetched. How disheartening it must be for God to have His word doubted. When God gave instructions to Gideon on how to defeat the Midianites, what do you think would have hindered him from obeying? The devil? Not necessarily. When God gives you a senseless instruction, your mind starts the battle of believing.

God's wisdom seeks peace, human wisdom seeks success and obviously, demonic wisdom seeks chaos! Godly wisdom is pure and seeks purity, human wisdom seeks to be happy irrespective of purity. When Godly wisdom is at work in your life, it will depict itself as humble as opposed to human wisdom which seeks to be praised and promotes self.

In conclusion, you can't be an effective extension of God here on earth without your tongue being tamed and you walking in the wisdom of God. These are the two major points Apostle James trashes out in this chapter.

Chapter Four
The World And Pride

If you noticed, Apostle James had started hinting on the topic of strife originating from jealousy and then bordering on fights and quarrels in the previous chapter. This is one reason he addressed the use of the tongue and of course, wisdom. Fights and quarrels were part of a bigger picture in the form of worldliness. In dealing with worldliness among God's people, Henry Drummond said, "Nothing exposes religion more to the reproach of its enemies than the worldliness and hard-heartedness of its professors." How true this is!

To prove that James knew why they had such issues in the church, he writes, "Where do wars and fights come from among you? Do they not come from your desires for pleasure that war in your members?" (James 4:1 NKJV). Taking a closer look at worldliness, you must understand that the moment you start conceiving the thoughts of you being satisfied rather than God, you're being worldly and need to check yourself quickly.

The world is controlled by a system that best suits its desires. This system is responsible for the structure and way of life of that world. So when James wrote about the worldliness that the church expressed, he was basically about the system that ran the world they lived in. This system is directly opposed to God's rule, desires, will, agenda and every other thing related to God and His kingdom; it is God's enemy! James bares his mind on this by writing, "Do you not know that friendship with the world id enmity with God? Whoever therefore wants to be a friend of the world makes himself an enemy of God." (James 4:4 NKJV). It grieved the Apostle that this system had crept into the church.

Worldliness is simply applying the thought-pattern and system of the world which is contrary to the life of God. In this world, anything and everything goes. You could desire something that belonged to someone else and not think it wrong to be envious. You could be so self-conscious that the feelings of others would matter less to you, as far as you got what you wanted. This would be okay in the world; the world would call you wise for "looking out for number one". Even if you murdered to get what you wanted, some people would be ready to give you a standing ovation. What a crazy world! This is the kind of life that had wormed its way into the lives of the Apostle's audience. But there's no way this is what God wants. Later James revealed what kind of character God actually wanted the church to have.

DESIRES AND PLEASURES

Although both words are frequently used interchangeably, they don't mean the same thing. Desires hinge more on the drive or pursuit after sin while pleasures are the derivative satisfaction that come after sin is found. Worldliness reveals itself in desires and pleasures. When evil seems to prevail in such a gathering, you should ask, "Why would there be such things as warring and fighting in the church?" Don't think too much, the desires and pleasures of people sponsors these fights and strife and characters of the world right there in the church. Sad!

The reason you could start a fight with someone is a hidden desire to try and prove to be better than that person. When someone has what you don't have, this could raise within you a strong desire to get it by all means. What do you think accounts for most of the wars in the world? One nation desperately wants what another nation enjoys, they'd rather try to take over the government of that country than partner peacefully. When your heart is set too much at something, you are likely not to hear clearly from God what His desires concerning it is.

James also wrote something interesting about praying for what you don't have. He wrote, "You ask and do not receive, because you ask amiss, that you may spend it on your pleasures." (James 4:3 NKJV). Although it is better to ask God for something because someone else has it than being jealous and fighting over it, the Apostle revealed that the reason such prayers would not be answered was the same reason another person would prefer to fight: pleasure! Worldliness is really a problem because instead of spending time seeking God's face for deeper and more intimate reasons, you'd be wasting time praying unanswerable prayers.

WAYS OUT

Apostle James did well not to only spell out their problems but also provided solutions to them. First, he writes, "But He gives us more and more grace (power of the Holy Spirit, to meet this evil tendency and all others fully). That is why He says, 'God sets Himself against the proud and haughty, but gives grace [continually] to the lowly (those who are humble enough to receive it).'" (James 4:6 AMP).

More and More Grace

There's definitely no way God would want you to do His will and not provide help. This help is in the form of a Spirit Being: The Holy Spirit. The Holy Spirit is He Who supplies grace to live above worldliness. This grace is also called strength in other versions of the same verse. This means that the moment you try to live in holiness by your own strength, you'll start failing.

Strength was the prayer Paul prayed for the church when he prayed that the church be strengthened with might in the inner man. The strength the Holy Spirit provides is first and foremost spiritual before physical. For example, a man would not only need spiritual strength to decline sexual sin but also need physical strength to flee from it as far as his legs can carry him.

Submission, the Formula.

Looking at James writing, we get a closer look at what submission to God involves. He writes, "Therefore submit to God. Resist the devil and he will flee from you." (James 4:7 NKJV). It's a formula! How? Simple, you can't do one without the other. Submitting to God comes first before resisting the devil; in this case, resisting the urge to give in to worldliness. Resisting the devil simply means to deny the devil access into your space; refusing to be led by him or any other form of association.

This is one major truth the church yet understood and it prompted the Apostle who loved them wholeheartedly to write to their reading. He made them understand that the reason they gave in to worldliness and its associated problems was that they'd not learned to give in to the will of God, they hadn't submitted themselves to God. For example, no man can heal the sick or work any other miracle with God's power without first submitting himself to God's authority; his case could end up like the seven sons of Sceva. Acts 19:14-17.

Come Closer

This was a call to fellowship! James knew that the reason worldliness crept in and caused problems was because they weren't spending time with God. Their fellowship with God was supposed to deal with the desires of the flesh.

James writes, "Draw near to God and He will draw near to you..." (vs. 8a NKJV). He even leaves a promise. Another formula! The more your draw close to God, the closer He'll get and the farther your worldly desires will be from you.

Wash Up!

Think of a drop of ink in a large container of clean, clear water. That little drop would make the whole body of water bad for use. Calling their attention to the matter of sanctification of the hands and heart, James wrote in the ending part of chapter 4 verse 8, "...Cleanse your hands, you sinners; and purify your hearts, you double-minded." (NKJV). Even though they were Christians, he called them sinners and double-minded. Why?

A sinner is someone who thinks and lives in line with the system that governs the world. A double-minded person says a resounding "YES!" but acts in the opposite. These people had accepted Jesus, but they were still acting like sinners in the world. Being worldly doesn't necessarily have to do with location; they expressed it even in the Church.

This is what prompted James to bring the topic of sanctification to them. In curing worldliness, one of the major things you must do is cleanse your heart and hands from every form of sin. You'll need to wash up!

But this wash up is not physically but spiritually. How possible would you cut out your heart to wash with soap, sponge and disinfectants? Or how would washing your hands physically cure a spiritual issue of worldliness? That's right, impossible! Washing off worldliness from you means spending time meditating on the Word of God and in prayers. By being consistent, you'll be flooding your heart with Godliness instead.

Godly Sorrow

Although James didn't use the phrase while writing, he revealed that sincere remorse for the strife, wars, envying and other acts of worldliness was a step in curing it. This kind of sorrow is what Peter felt after denying Jesus the third time and realized his wrong.

There was no way James was going to write his heart out without addressing their disposition towards their misbehaviors. He writes even to you when you see yourself living worldly that you should, "Lament and mourn and weep! Let your laughter be turned to mourning and your joy to gloom." (James 4:9 NKJV).

Godly sorrow leads to genuine repentance and a resolution to live upright afterwards (2 Corinthians 7:10). James' main aim for writing was for the church to repent in thoughts, words and deeds of every wrongdoing he got wind of.

HUMILITY

> "Sin came through the pride of Lucifer and salvation came through the humility of Jesus."
>
> - Zac Poonen

You've probably heard that humility is one of those virtues that when you think you have it, you start losing it. You can't say anything like, "Wow, I admire my humility!" I'm really humble! That's not how it works. Have you seen people who boast about how humble they are? Look at them closely.

According to him, the issue was selfishness of people. He implied that they weren't considering the good of the entire body of Christ. Think about it, sometimes you find yourself in the shoes of these people. When you're not humble, it means you're not considering the greater benefit. You're preoccupied with your own selfish desires. You are battling and contending with others because you want your own way. Isn't it always the case when there's a disagreement? We constantly want to do things our way.

This kind of life is a sharp contrast to humility. Humility is you living life with the consciousness that you are and have nothing except what God's makes and gives you. This consciousness is meant to make you break the hold of the feeling of entitlement to anything. By doing this, you'll be setting yourself up to be lifted by the Lifter of men Himself. It is the same thing James writes, "Humble yourselves in the sight of the Lord, and He will lift you up." (James 4:10 NKJV).

Take a cue from Jesus Who used the greatest level of humility to save the world. Paul writes, "... (Jesus) made Himself of no reputation, taking the form of a bondservant, and coming in the likeness of men." (Philippians 2:7 NKJV). The singular fact that He became flesh and blood was enough to give Him the highest accolades of humility. When you make yourself of no reputation before God and men, you'll neither envy nor fight anyone for anything. And before you even ask for yours from a sincere heart, God will hear and answer.

Chapter Five
Justice, Prayer, And Mercy

The Apostle James ends his epistle with a fifth chapter which he begins by echoing God's judgment upon those who abuse the poor. He made sure to reveal to their faces how grievous their sins were before God. In the first six verse, he states how severe their punishments would be. He aimed at reminding them of such a phenomenon as justice and that God is the perfect judge!

James also wrote to those who were going through one trial or the other, exhorting them to be patient and remain faithful till the end. Still bringing back the issue of the tongue being misused, he warned against swearing and instructed on how to respond to situations regarding adversity and wealth.

The Apostle then writes about prayers for the sick and anointing with oil. Still on prayer, he writes about Christians confessing faults and praying to and for each other respectively, proving the efficacy of prayer. He lastly writes about how a fallen brother can be restored to God and the fold. Let's dig in, shall we?

YOU RICH MEN!
Apostle James thought it best to address the rich men. He wrote, "Come now, you rich, weep and howl for your miseries that are coming upon you." (James 5:1 NKJV). This must have been strange because

they were not necessarily Christians and could most likely not read his epistle. Even if they were not active in the church, they would be the greedy affluent people. They were most likely the unbelieving Jews who were worldly. What happened here was that most of the less privileged Jews received Christ and His teachings as well as His way of life. This was the opposite for most of the rich Jews; they rejected Christianity. They had hardened their hearts against the Gospel and hated the Jews who weren't on their side.

Another angle to this would be of those Christians who were spiritually rich. This means that these people were spiritually strong and had enjoyed deep dimensions of God more than so many other Christians. This would make them puff up with pride and make others feel less important to God. The Apostle couldn't have left them out in these first six verses.

Either way, James warns that if they didn't repent, they would experience what he called 'misery'. Even you wouldn't want to think of what that could mean. This tells of how terrible the sin of oppression and pride could be to the church. He asked them to weep and howl which didn't express a causal grief. He wrote in second verse, "Your riches are corrupted, and your garments are moth-eaten." (James 5:2 NKJV). What could be more devastating than heaping wealth that would only be eaten by moths? You wouldn't want to be in their shoes.

This same warning is what the Apostle gives you if you in any way or at any time oppress those who are not apparently as privileged as you are. It would really be a thing of sorrow if God blesses you, but you allow pride and oppression get in the way of you being a blessing to others in return. Just as James seemed to advise them to have godly sorrow if perhaps their misery would be averted, you must have a posture of conviction that God is displeased when you act like these rich men.

Looking closely at the 'misery' the Apostle writes about, there are several descriptions he gives. He writes about these riches with which people oppress others would decay and rotten with time. He also writes that the garments of these rich oppressors would be destroyed by moths. Because of this terrible character, James revealed that their gold and silver would rust; of course, he knew these two metals could never really rust, he meant that they would lose value inevitably. James proceeded to write about the physical implication of this 'misery that would come'; the judgment would afflict their actual bodies.

If you're not careful, you may open yourself and everyone around you to become prone to destruction as a result of you oppressing the poor. Although he wrote to the unbelieving rich, this very much concerns you because at some point, you may have fallen into the trap of looking down on those who aren't 'at your level'.

UNTIL THE COMING OF THE LORD.

To be patient means to suffer long and this is a step up the ladder of patience. What makes it patience is that it is void of complaints and desires to repay wrongs done to you. You'll understand when you the write that this patience is until Jesus comes. James shifted focus from the rich oppressors to those Christians who were facing one trying time of their lives or the other. He writes, "Therefore be patient, brethren, until the coming of the Lord. See how the farmer waits for the precious fruit of the earth, waiting patiently for it until it receives the early and latter rain." (James 5:7 NKJV). This may not necessarily mean rapture. It could mean whenever God decides to intervene in a situation.

When you going through a situation, think of the fact that God is aware, and your secured victory requires that you wait patiently for His intervention. Interesting how the Apostle uses the illustration of a farmer who patiently waits for the fruit of his labor over a plant. It would be better to understand what waiting would take. First, a vision! How? If you will wait patiently on God, you must have conditioned your mind to see things through the eyes of God; the eyes of faith! This is what the farmer does; before he plants, he has already seen his seed growing into a massive tree. It is what pushes him to plant in the first place.

This is what Job saw; he knew his God enough to make such a statement as, "Though He slay me, yet will I trust Him..." (Job 13:15 NKJV). If there's anyone in the Bible who understood what it meant to wait patiently, it was Job. Job's life took a complete turn for the worst when he lost all his wealth and ten children in one day. Yes, one day! How he didn't run mad or faint or commit suicide is a mystery in itself. If he lost everything within the course of ten years or so, you would still feel pity for him. But how does someone lose everything in one day? As if that was not enough, he lost his health too. He became an epitome of wretchedness in a rather short time!

But in all he went through, a testimony about him was that through all, he said nothing wrong against God. The text says, as he scolded his wife for asking him to curse God and die, "In all this, Job did not sin with his lips." (Job 2:10 NKJV). Even if you have the right to say the wrong things in your time of pain, being patient with words is the way to go! James writes in the very first chapter, "So then, my beloved brethren, let every man be...slow to speak." (James 1:19 NKJV). When you're faced with difficult situations, or someone annoys you or something happens that grieves you, be careful not to let your first response be ill words. It's better to be quiet than to say the wrong things when you're hurting.

Have you been faced with a disheartening situation, and you feel God isn't on your side or at least He's partnered with your enemies? How have you handled those times, well? Did your disposition towards God at those points depict trust in Him or doubt in His intentions for you? What did you say in those times? Can you, like Job, not sin with your lips in those painful moments of loss? Did you think Job's patience did not pay off in the end? Did his Lord not come? He sure did! Job was blessed twice as much as he had before his affliction. And He's coming to you, but if only you'll see Him as He does.

Another example of people who persevered and waited patiently for the coming of the Lord were the prophets. They went through terrible times as they stood for God. Speaking for God alone took them to their graves. They were ready to die for the cause of God to be pushed against the system of the world. James wrote, "My brethren, take the prophets, who spoke in the name of the Lord, as an example of suffering and patience." (James 5:10 NKJV).

THE MATTER OF PRAYER

Truly, the topic of prayer can't be overemphasized and James aimed at recommending the positions that should be taken in times of afflictions and rejoicing. He writes, "Is anyone among you suffering? Let him pray. Is anyone cheerful? Let his sing psalms." (James 5:13 NKJV). Recall that the Apostle had begun the epistle by writing about suffering and encouragement to rejoice in every circumstance. It isn't only in bad times you pray. At all times, thanksgiving which is part of the model prayer given by Jesus (Luke 11:2-4) should be made.

The Answer to Affliction

Unlike so many popular beliefs, prayer is the answer to affliction. This affliction isn't just when you're having a bad day or a fall out with a loved one. According to James, these afflictions were like the ones the prophets went through while choosing to stand with God and opposing the evil world. These prophets were persecuted for speaking God's word and contending with the world and they paid the price; some, the ultimate price.

James made sure his readers understood enough what the prophets went through and what their dispositions were. He wrote to confirm that as hard at it was; prayer was and is the solution to times of affliction. When you're faced with tough times, don't make the mistake of cringing in your shell of self-pity. No! It never helps. It's rather a time to get on your knees and let Him take the wheel.

No doubt tough times will come, but what proves your Christianity is your response in those times. Do you remember when the Apostles and Christians were persecuted by the sect of the Sanhedrin? What did they do first? That's right, they prayed for boldness. (Acts 4:29-31). They didn't even pray for God to stop the persecution or deliver them. They were too occupied rejoicing for being counted worthy to be persecuted for Christ's sake! They prayed for boldness to face these tough times. You may need to go through your afflictions so that like gold tried in fire, you'll come out of it valuable! But make sure you're engaging He who knows all things and can help you.

The Solution to Sickness

In case anyone thought James didn't care about those who could be physically afflicted or having health issues as their tough time, he wrote, "Is anyone among you sick? Let him call for the elders of the church, and let them pray over him, anointing him with oil in the name of the Lord." (vs. 14 NKJV). He was most likely referring to chronic illnesses that would require the sick one to be bedridden. Calling for the elders didn't necessarily mean that the elders had the power to heal but they represented the church. Praying for the sick could heal the person, not 'will'. James wasn't promising but was in a way promoting love and responsibility.

When your body fails you and gives in to physical illnesses that restrain your movement, you'll do well to reach out to brethren in the Lord. These people are meant to join faith with you to receive your healing. That's right, 'receive'. Prayer isn't asking for what hasn't happened but asking for the manifestation of what has happened in the spirit realm through Christ. Your times of sickness are not for you to push God aside or give excuses for not fellowshipping with your heavenly Father; they are rather one of the best times to engage God for those realities made possible in Christ.

In Trespasses

James thought it best to address spiritual sickness next. He wrote about the disposition towards sin and confession. He wrote, "Confess your trespasses to one another, and pray for one another, that you may be healed. The effective, fervent prayer of a righteous man avails much." (James 5:16 NKJV). You're to confess your sins and faults to people in the church you trust to understand are ready to help you out as God gives grace. After this is done, prayers can be made for and by each other. When you fall into sin or do something wrong, the first people that you should reach out to for help are people of like-minds of seeing God glorified.

THE PRAYER OF THE RIGHTEOUS

One of the first things we notice about the prophet Elijah was his prayer life. This was what James aimed at when he referenced the fiery prophet of God. He started by reminding his readers that Elijah was as much human as anyone on the street but his being a prophet wasn't really the reason his prayer life was red-hot. The most prominent situation that proves he was a man of prayer was when there was no rain in the land of Israel for three years and six months (his doing).

The story in the Old Testament (1 Kings 18:42-46) reveals that when Elijah prayed for the rain to come, his servant whom he sent to check if his prayers had been answered came back six times disappointed. It was the seventh time that his prayers were answered! Have you prayed for the same thing for seven times before? It's not likely to keep praying for the same thing after the third time of no answer; but like Elijah, James encourages you to stay there, persevering and being consistent until answers come.

Saving Souls

James wraps up his entire epistle by writing about saving the soul of anyone who wanders from the faith. He made it clear that it was everyone's responsibility to see that lost souls were restored from the clutches of death. He wrote, "Brethren, if anyone among you wanders from the truth, and someone turns him back, let him know that he who turns a soul from death and cover a multitude of sins." (James 5:19-20 NKJV).

Although it is the primary work of pastors or shepherds to bring back lost souls, it is everyone's assignment as earlier revealed by Paul in 2 Corinthians 5:18. Sometimes, you may be privy to know Christians who have fallen into one error or the other, it's your responsibility to help them out of that fallen state. It is never a time to condemn or judge them, but a time to identify with their weaknesses and God's strength and praying with them. By doing this, you'll be saving their souls as Christ has endorsed and commanded and as James instructs.